BEFORE YOU BEGIN...

Make sure to download the FREE audio program for this book which comes with your purchase! Just go to

www.slangman.com/audio

then look for your book and enter this code:

E2J1L8ALCWN7

Book Design and Production: Slangman Publishing.

Written by: David Burke
Copy Editor: Julie Bobrick
Illustrated by: "Migs!" Sandoval
Translator: Mariko Bird

Copyright © 2017 by David Burke

Email: info@heywordy.com
Website: www.heywordy.com

Hey Wordy! and all related characters and elements are © and trademarks of Hey Wordy, LLC.

Published by Slangman Publishing. Slangman is a registered trademark of David Burke. All rights reserved. Reproduction or translation of any part of this work beyond that permitted by section 107 or 108 of the 1976 United States Copyright Act without the permission of the copyright owner is unlawful. Requests for permission or further information should be addressed to the Permissions Department, Slangman Publishing. This publication is designed to provide accurate and authoritative information in regard to the subject matter covered. The persons, entities and events in this book are fictitious. Any similarities with actual persons or entities, past and present, are purely coincidental.

ISBN13: 978-1-891888-51-9

Printed in the U.S.A.

Meet the Author
David Burke

Creator and star of the children's TV show, *Hey Wordy!*, David Burke has been single-handedly revolutionizing the foreign language-learning movement worldwide.

In addition to being a performer of boundless energy and enthusiasm, David speaks seven languages. A successful author and entrepreneur, he has built a thriving international publishing company featuring over 100 books he has written for teen/adults & children. His books have won publishing awards and have sold more than one million copies. David's Street Speak™ and Biz Speak™ series of books and audio programs are used around the world by government agencies, leading universities and major corporations.

Since age 4, David has been a classically trained pianist and uses his musical gifts to compose and perform original songs for his TV series, *Hey Wordy!* which introduces children to foreign languages and cultures through music, animation, and magical adventures. He has also composed, orchestrated, and performed all the music in the audio programs for each of these books.

David's engaging and charismatic persona became a fixture on broadcast entertainment channels around the world, such as CNN and the BBC. David and his work have been highlighted in many major publications, including The Los Angeles Times, The Chicago Tribune and The Christian Science Monitor.

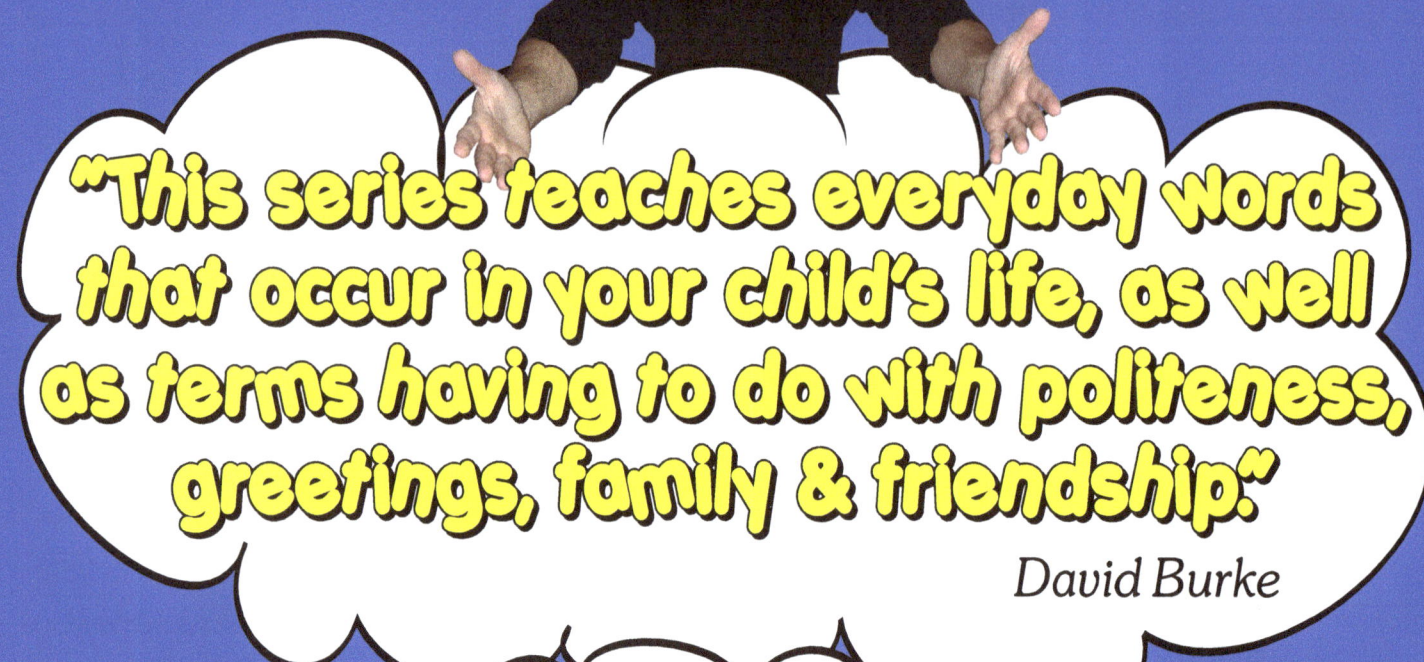

"This series teaches everyday words that occur in your child's life, as well as terms having to do with politeness, greetings, family & friendship."

David Burke

Japanese vocabulary taught:

aishteru = in love
arigato = thank you
ashee = foot
chotto-no-aida = moment
doita-shimashteh = you're welcome
doresu = dress
eejeewaru = mean
hansamna = handsome
kanashee = sad
kawa-ee = pretty

kutsu = shoe
mahyonaka = midnight
ojisama = prince
okeena = big
oksan = wife
onanoko = girl
pahtee = party
sayonara = goodbye
shiawaseh = happy
yeh = house

Dedication

The entire "Foreign Language Through Fairy Tales" series is dedicated to all the children of the world.

It is through their understanding, appreciation, and celebration of our differences that the world will become a better and safer place for us all.

onanoko
おんなのこ
kawa-ee
かわいい

yeh
いえ

Once upon a time, there lived a girl named Cinderella who was very pretty. The **kaw-ee onanoko** lived in a small house with her stepmother and

two stepsisters. At times it was difficult for the **kawa-ee onanoko** to live in such a small **yeh** with her stepmother and stepsisters. Why? Because they were

eejeewaru
いじわる

jealous that she was so **kawa-ee** which is why her stepmother was extra mean to her. But the **kawa-ee onanoko** never complained about living in a small

yeh with her **eejeewaru** stepmother and two stepsisters, even though they forced her to do all the work in the entire **yeh** day in and day out!

pahtee
パーティー

okeena
おおきな

One day, a royal invitation arrived at the **yeh** of the **kawa-ee onanoko**. The king was throwing a party for the prince. And the **pahtee** was going to be big.

An **okeena pahtee**! The prince was very handsome and it was at this **okeena pahtee** that the **hansamna** prince hoped to find the **kawa-ee** wife he had been seeking.

hansamna
ハンサムな

oksan
おくさん

7

ojisama
おうじさま

The king and queen also hoped the **hansamna prince** would find a **kawa-ee oksan** at the **okeena pahtee** because they wanted the **hansamna ojisama** to be very happy.

The night of the **okeena pahtee** arrived but Cinderella was sad – very **kanashee** because her **eejeewaru** stepmother wouldn't let her leave the **yeh**!

kanashee
かなしい

9

Poor, **kanashee** Cinderella had to stay in her **yeh** and never get the chance to meet the **hansamna ojisama** at the **okeena pahtee** and become his **oksan**.

Then she heard a voice say, "My dear, I'm your fairy godmother and you'll be able to go to the **okeena pahtee** and you'll be wearing a **kawa-ee** dress!"

doresu
ドレス

Arigato
ありがとう

And with a wave of her magic wand, Cinderella was now wearing a **kawa-ee doresu** made of the finest silk. "Oh, Thank you! **Arigato**!" exclaimed Cinderella. She was a **kawa-ee**

onanoko wearing a **kawa-ee doresu**, and eager to leave her **yeh** to go meet the **hansamna ojisama** at the **okeena pahtee** in hopes of becoming his **oksan**!

13

chotto-no-aida
ちょっとのあいだ

mahyon-aka
まよなか

"One moment!" the fairy godmother added. "Make sure to leave the **okeena pahtee** by midnight because your **kawa-ee doresu** will change back to what it was!" Cinderella

thought for a **chotto-no-aida** then said, "I'll remember to leave before **mahyonaka**." And with that, the **kawa-ee onanoko** left for the **okeena pahtee**. She was

15

shiawaseh
しあわせ

no longer **kanashee**, but very happy to be meeting the **hansamna ojisama**. As she got out of her carriage, she could hear the **okeena pahtee**! Cinderella walked in

and wasn't too **shiawaseh** to see more than one **kawa-ee onanoko** waiting to meet the **hansamna ojisama**. But after a **chotto-no-aida**, she calmed down and was ready to

17

meet the **hansamna ojisama** face to face. And **hansamna** he was! She could hardly believe her eyes! And it was clear the **hansamna ojisama** was in love with

aishteru
あいしてる

the **kawa-ee onanoko** the very first **chotto-no-aida** he saw her! "**Arigato** for inviting me" said Cinderella. "You're welcome" responded the **hansamna ojisama**.

Doita-shimashteh
どういたしまして

They danced for hours, until the stroke of **mahyonaka** was upon them which the **kawa-ee onanoko** had completely forgotten about! *Poof!* Her **kawa-ee doresu** vanished!

"Goodbye!" shouted Cinderella. "**Sayonara**! And **arigato** again for inviting me!" "**Doitashimashteh**," responded the **hansamna ojisama**. And Cinderella ran back to her **yeh**.

Sayonara
さようなら

21

kutsu くつ

The only thing she left behind was a glass shoe. The **hansamna ojisama** was extremely **kanashee** and went from town to town looking for a **kawa-ee onanoko**

ashee
あし

whose foot would fit the glass **kutsu**. After days of eliminating **onanoko** after **onanoko**, the **hansamna ojisama** was even more **kanashee** than ever, but he

23

had one more **yeh** to visit. The **eejeewaru** stepmother ran out to see if her **ashee** would fit the glass **kutsu**. The two stepsisters followed behind. But it was no use. He still couldn't find

an **ashee** to fit the **kutsu**! The **hansamna ojisama** was **kanashee** and about to give up, but at that very **chotto-no-aida**, he spotted Cinderella standing by the **yeh**.

There was something special about her. He just had to see if her **ashee** was the one that could fit the glass **kutsu**. He knelt down in front of her and slid the **kutsu** on her **ashee**.

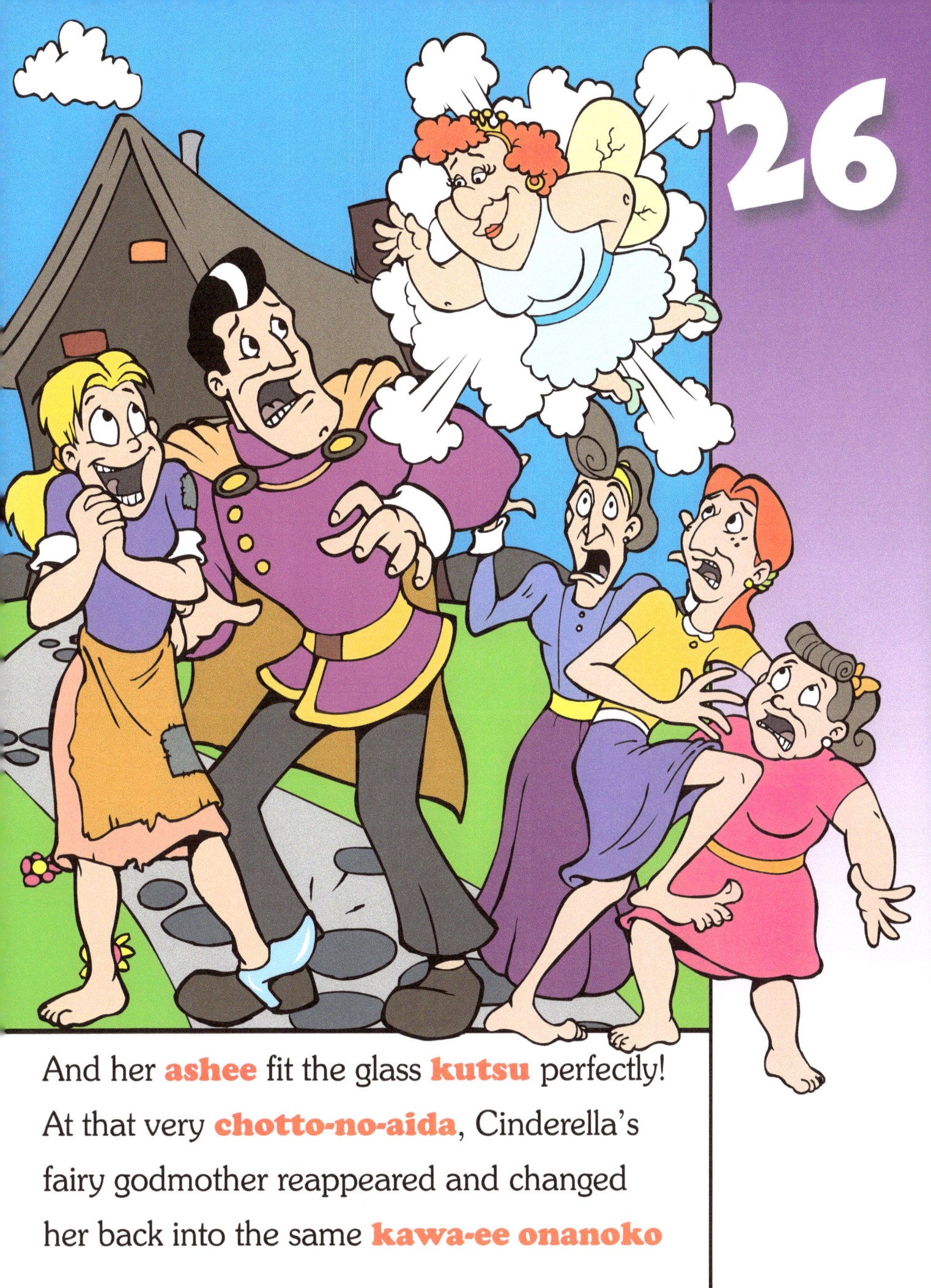

And her **ashee** fit the glass **kutsu** perfectly! At that very **chotto-no-aida**, Cinderella's fairy godmother reappeared and changed her back into the same **kawa-ee onanoko**

in the **kawa-ee doresu** the **hansamna ojisama** had met at his **okeena pahtee**. He was now more **aishteru** than ever! The **kawa-ee onanoko** was **shiawaseh**

that she lost her glass **kutsu** at the **okeena pahtee** or the **hansamna ojisama** may never have found her! Soon, Cinderella became his **oksan**. She was so very

shiawaseh! She would never, ever be **kanashee** again. And the **hansamna ojisama** and the **kawa-ee onanoko**, Cinderella, lived in the castle happily ever after.

Now you're ready for Level 2!

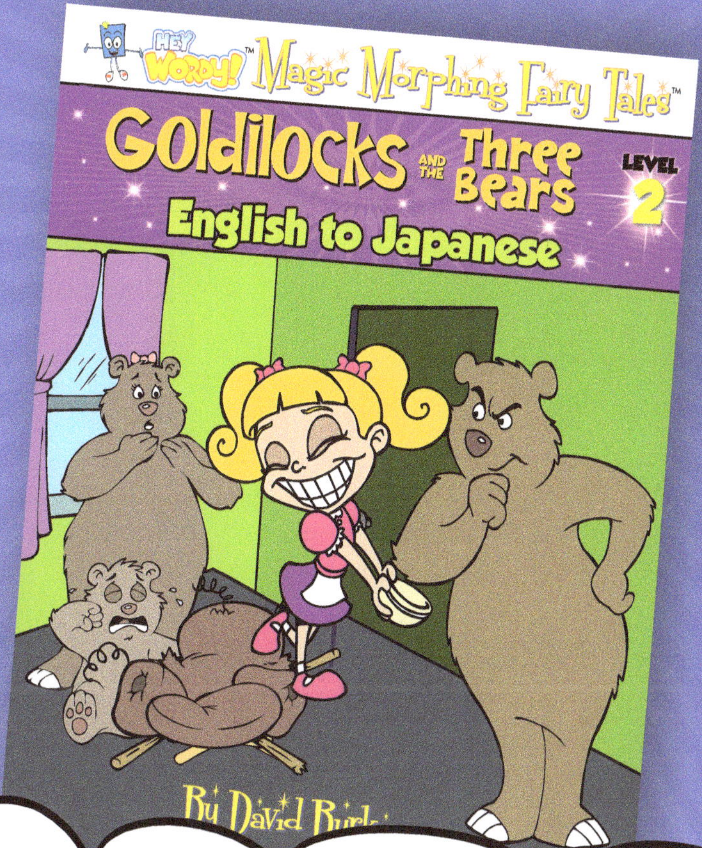

Goldilocks and the Three Bears — English to Japanese — LEVEL 2

Magic Morphing Fairy Tales

By David Burke

Level 2 contains words from Level 1, plus all NEW words!

For more HEY WORDY! products, visit...

www.ingramcontent.com/pod-product-compliance
Lightning Source LLC
Chambersburg PA
CBHW040508110526
44587CB00047B/4372